Pag

Part IV: Vafþrú & [?]

Óðinn in Yggdrasill

By Varg Vikernes & Marie Cachet

Initial Notes

In this booklet we will look at original sources and what they say about Valhöll and then explain what it means. We will also explain the myth about Óðinn sacrificing himself in the Tree of Life.

Varg Vikernes
June 2018

Grímnismál

Most of what we know about Valhöll comes from some of the stanzas of Grímnismál, and then this is supported by what is said in The Younger Edda. Normally the stanzas of the myths are only partly translated by the scholars, because all the *names* are left untranslated. Often the stanzas listing the names of the rivers and horses (and in other poems dwarves) are even left out completely. Because they make no sense to them. "It's just a list of names."

In 1998 I finished the book *Germansk Mytologi og Verdenanskuelse* ("Germanic Mythology and World View") where I actually translated also the names in the mythology. Amazingly, nobody else had done that before! This was a very time-consuming and tedious task that took several years to complete, and although the book itself is littered with misconceptions it proved to be a huge leap forward for our understanding of mythology. It showed for the first time that *the names themselves are the keys to understanding the mythology.*

So when I translate the stanzas below into English, I will also translate the names, when I can (some few names have an unknown meaning), and thus enable us to actually *understand* what Grímnismál is telling us. First of all though, I will list the original Norse stanzas dealing with Valhöll:

8. Glaðsheimr heitir inn fimmti,
þars in gullbjarta Valhöll víð of þrumir;
en þar Hroftr kýss hverjan dag
vápndauða vera.

9. Mjök er auðkennt,
þeim er til Óðins koma
salkynni at séa;
sköftum er rann reft,
skjöldum er salr þakiðr,
brynjum um bekki strát.

10. Mjök er auðkennt,
þeir er til Óðins koma
salkynni at séa:
vargr hangir fyr vestan dyrr,
ok drúpir örn yfir.
18. Andhrímnir lætr í Eldhrímni
Sæhrímni soðinn, fleska bezt;
en þat fáir vitu,
við hvat einherjar alask.

19. Gera ok Freka seðr gunntamiðr
hróðigr Herjaföður;
en við vín eitt vápngöfugr
Óðinn æ lifir.

20. Huginn ok Muninn fljúga hverjan dag
Jörmungrund yfir;
óumk ek of Hugin, at hann aftr né komi-t,
þó sjámk meir of Munin.

21. Þýtr Þund, unir Þjóðvitnis
fiskr flóði í;
árstraumr þykkir ofmikill
Valglaumni at vaða.

22. Valgrind heitir, er stendr velli á
heilög fyr helgum dyrum;
forn er sú grind, en þat fáir vitu,
hvé hon er í lás of lokin.

23. Fimm hundruð dura ok umb fjórum
tögum,
svá hygg ek á Valhöllu vera;
átta hundruð Einherja ganga senn ór einum
durum,
þá er þeir fara við vitni at vega.

24. Fimm hundruð golfa ok umb fjórum
tögum,
svá hygg ek Bilskirrni með bugum;
ranna þeira, er ek reft vita,
míns veit ek mest magar.

25. Heiðrún heitir geit, er stendr höllu á
ok bítr af Læraðs limum;
skapker fylla hon skal ins skíra mjaðar;
kná-at sú veig vanask.

26. Eikþyrnir heitir hjörtr, er stendr höllu á
ok bítr af Læraðs limum;
en af hans hornum drýpr í Hvergelmi,
þaðan eigu vötn öll vega.

27. Síð ok Víð, Sækin ok Eikin,
Svöl ok Gunnþró, Fjörm ok Fimbulþul,
Rín ok Rennandi, Gipul ok Göpul,
Gömul ok Geirvimul, þær hverfa um hodd
goða,
Þyn ok Vín, Þöll ok Höll, Gráð ok
Gunnþorin.

28. Vína heitir ein, önnur Vegsvinn,
þriðja Þjóðnuma, Nyt ok Nöt,
Nönn ok Hrönn, Slíð ok Hríð,
Sylgr ok Ylgr, Víð ok Ván,
Vönd ok Strönd, Gjöll ok Leiftr,
þær falla gumnum nær, er falla til Heljar
heðan.

29. Körmt ok Örmt ok Kerlaugar tvær,
þær skal Þórr vaða dag hvern,
er hann dæma ferr at aski Yggdrasils,
því at ásbrú brenn öll loga,
heilög vötn hlóa.

30. Glaðr ok Gyllir, Glær ok Skeiðbrimir, Silfrintoppr ok Sinir, Gísl ok Falhófnir, Gulltoppr ok Léttfeti, þeim ríða æsir jóm dag hvern, er þeir dæma fara at aski Yggdrasils.

Normally stanzas 27 to 30 are not believed to be related to Valhöll, but I will show you that they indeed are.

Óðinn in the Sacred Tree

We can start by explaining why it is called Valhöll. This is generally believed to be "The Hall of the Fallen", and scholars compare it to the Judeo-Christian eternal "Heavenly Paradise", claiming it is the "Paradise" of the Norsemen, where only those who died in combat would come. If you translate the name though, you will find that it can also translate as "Hall of the Chosen". Norse *valr* means "the fallen in a battle", but Norse *val* means "selection", "choosing" and "assortment". So it can be the hall of the fallen, but also the hall of the ones that have been selected.... but selected for what? And by whom?

Let us jump right into the translation and also the explanation to what the verses mean.

8. Glaðsheimr heitir inn fimmti,
þars in gullbjarta Valhöll víð of þrumir;
en þar Hroftr kýss hverjan dag
vápndauða vera.

8. The fifth is Glaðsheimr ("Fair Home"),
gold-bright there stands wide Valhöll;.
And there does Hroftr each day choose
men who have been killed with weapons.

Glaðsheimr is the home of Óðinn. Hroftr - a name for Óðinn - *might* mean "Sage", but it has no certain meaning. So at first glance it seems as if Óðinn, calling himself Hroftr here for some reason, sits in his "Heaven" and lets those who were killed with weapons come to his hall. This is what the scholars have told us, right? This is *the* Valhöll cliché. The Warrior's Paradise.

But what and who is Óðinn? And why would he care if you were killed with weapons or not? Because of Honour, right? It is more honourable for a man to die in battle than in bed. Ok, we can agree, but *what is* Honour? And more importantly: how did our forebears see it and *why* was it so important? Because they wanted to go to Valhöll? But what if you had great Honour and were *not* killed by weapons? You would then not go to Valhöll - if we are to take the stanza and what it says literally. And that doesn't make much sense does it? Who cares about *how you die*, if you lived an Honourable life!? But if we take it literally, a great warrior who fights and survives for decades, only to die e. g. by accidentally tripping over something and hitting his head, would *not* go to Valhöll, but some coward who has never seen battle in his life is accidentally killed by a hunter's spear (a weapon), he will?

Something is amiss here. Something is not right about the official version of this.

But before we continue let us have a look at Óðinn. Like I said, what and who is he? The king of the gods, Frigg's husband, Baldr's father, etc. etc. etc. Fine, but what if we actually take a look at the Óðinn myth that best defines Óðinn, namely Hávamál, and in particular stanza 138-139, where he hangs himself in the sacred tree, falls down and picks up the runes? Let's do that first of all, and see if we can from these stanzas understand better who and what Óðinn is:

From Hávamál:

Stanza 138.
Veit ek, at ek hekk
vindga meiði á
nætr allar níu,
geiri undaðr
ok gefinn Óðni,
sjalfr sjalfum mér,
á þeim meiði,
er manngi veit
hvers af rótum renn.

138.
I trow I hung,
on the windy tree
nights all nine,
with spear wounded
and given to Óðinn,
myself given to myself,
in that tree
that nobody knows
of what roots it runs.

139.
Við hleifi mik sældu
né við hornigi;
nýsta ek niðr,
nam ek upp rúnar,
æpandi nam,
fell ek aftr þaðan.

139.
No bread they gave me
nor drink from a horn,
I looked down,
picked up secrets,
took them and screamed,
yet again I fell from there.

Many like to see this as some sort of heroic self-sacrifice for deeper spiritual knowledge, achieved through suffering and fasting. They like to think that the rune signs came about this way: he picked them up from the ground and then he finally fell from the tree.

But why did he fall? Why did he hang there for nine nights? Why was he wounded with a spear? Why didn't he eat or drink from a horn? How could he survive nine nights without drinking? How could he even give himself to himself? What does that even mean? How could he pick up the runes *before* he fell? And why did he fall *again*? Had he fallen already!? If so, why didn't he pick up the runes (before?) the first time he fell? When did he fall the first time? How many times has he fallen from that tree, and why isn't there anything about those other times in the myths?!

We can bury ourselves in questions like these, and dig deep into the absurd, or we can realize that this poem is *not* about an old one-eyed god who hangs himself in a tree. He is a *symbol* with a deeper meaning.

Yes. We need to think symbols here. What is it Óðinn *symbolizes* in our mythology? If he is not some old one-eyed god riding around on an eight-legged horse, then what is it he symbolizes?

In fact, we need to realize that *everything* in the myths are symbols! Not just the named gods and places, trees and ettins and whatever. Everything is a symbol with a deeper meaning, and not least, everything is there for a reason. Óðinn. The tree of life. Nine days. The spear. Not eating. Not drinking from a horn. Falling. Picking up the secrets. Everything means something *else*. Everything symbolizes something else!

Thankfully, our forebears made that very clear to us, because if the myths *don't* mean something *else*, if they don't have a hidden meaning, then... they make *no* sense! They show us *the impossible*, so that we shall understand that *there is something else here*. Or do you really think that they made impossible stories that we were supposed to believe in? Wagons pulled by goats flying through the sky? Hammers that return to your hand when you throw it? Gods transforming into mares and giving birth to an eight-legged horse that can fly? Really?

If you believe that this is what our mythology tells us, and that this is what our forebears believed in, then I have some news for you: It doesn't. They didn't.

So let us find out what these symbols mean....

The name Óðinn translates as "Mind", "Thought" and "Excited State of Mind". It can also mean "Mad", "Wild", "Furious" and "Eager", but it's meaning is mainly and first of all "Mind". The tree he hangs himself in is not a real tree, but the placenta: it looks like a tree though, and it gives life. Óðinn is the "father of the gods", and he attaches himself to the tree of life with a spear: to the placenta with the umbilical cord. The "nine nights" are the nine solar months of pregnancy. Naturally, he does not eat anything there, whilst in the womb of the mother. He does not drink from any horns whilst there either. He gets all his nourishment via the umbilical cord.

Óðinn is the Mind... that is being *re-incarnated*. He is the sum of all the forebears, "the father of all the gods", in one symbol.

"...given to Óðinn,
myself given to myself..."

His Mind is poured into the new physical body, the child, the fetus, from the tree of life, as it is created in the womb of the mother.

From Völuspá, stanza 28:

Allt veit ek, Óðinn,
hvar þú auga falt,
í inum mæra
Mímisbrunni.
Drekkr mjöð Mímir
morgun hverjan
af veði Valföðrs.
Vituð ér enn - eða hvat?

All I know, Óðinn,
where your eye is hidden,
in the famous well of Mímir
Every morning
Mímir mead drinks
from the father of the chosen's pledge.
Do you still not know enough or what?

Ah, but you have been told by the scholars
that Óðinn has only one eye, right? Well, he
does not. That is of course also a symbol for
something else. His "one eye in the well of
Mímir", that he had to sacrifice for
knowledge, is his belly button... when he is

in the womb of the mother it is connected to the umbilical cord – his spear, alias Mímir's well. That long well that connects him to the tree of life.

Oh, I guess it's time to translate the name Mímir for you: "Reminiscence"! Which of course is defined as "the act or process of recalling past experiences, events, etc."

I told you he was re-incarnating, but to recall past lives, and become himself again, himself given to himself, he needs to connect to the tree of life, that we also know as Mímir's head. His learning process starts in the womb of the mother, and he learns *from the placenta*.

Funnily enough, that is *exactly* what happens too.... the placenta is instrumental in activating genes in the fetus, in giving it life, in creating the child. Like an architect for a building. No matter the amount of materials you have at your hand: No architect, no functional building.

Then finally he is born:

"I looked down,
picked up secrets,
took them and screamed,
yet again I fell from there."

He picked up the runes (secrets) *before* he fell, because they represent what he learnt from Mímir, based on previous lives. He falls *again*, because he was *re-born*. Óðinn returns to life. He re-incarnates!

....and he is not some old one-eyed god riding an eight-legged horse that can fly through the air. He is the sum of your forebears! He is you. He is your Mind!

You still don't know enough, or what?

Mímameiðr

Let us continue. Where is the connection between Mímir and Yggdrasill? Did I just make that up? Did I over-interpret things here? No, everything is in our mythology, plain and clear, right in front of our eyes. In Fjölsvinnsmál stanza 20 we learn that:

20.
Mímameiðr hann heitir,
en þat manngi veit,
af hverjum rótum renn;
við þat hann fellr,
er fæstan varir,
flær-at hann eld né járn.

20.
Is called Mímameiðr
not many know,
where the roots run,
or how it is felled,
few know,
neither fire nor axe bites it.

Mímameiðr is another name for Yggdrasill, and what does it translate as? "The Tree of Mímir". It is the placenta transferring past experiences to the fetus. Therefore we learn that Óðinn is drinking from the well of Mímir.

Let us talk some more about Yggdrasill before we continue. Because some symbols related to Yggdrasill have not been explained here.

Völuspá, stanza 19:

19.
Ask veit ek standa,
heitir Yggdrasill,
hár baðmr, ausinn
hvíta auri;
þaðan koma döggvar,
þærs í dala falla,
stendr æ yfir grænn
Urðarbrunni.

19.
I know an ash stand
is called Yggdrasill
it stands tall,
wet from white water,
from it comes the dew
that falls in the valleys
stands forever green above the well of Urðr.

Urðr translates as "Honour", but is commonly seen as being the norn of the past. Past honour. Again the term "Honour"... we will return to that later on.

And what is it that creates the water in the womb, wherein the fetus lie, whilst being nourished by the placenta? Yes, the amniotic bag. Drops of dew drips over the placenta. Over Yggdrasill.

Grímnismál:

32.

Ratatoskr heitir íkorni,
er renna skal
at aski Yggdrasils,
arnar orð
hann skal ofan bera
ok segja Niðhöggvi niðr.

32.

The squirrel is called Ratatoskr
he shall run,
on the ash Yggdrasill.
The words of the eagle
he shall carry from above
and bring down to Niðhöggr.

Ratatoskr means "run about", and we actually see his name explained right after he is mentioned in the stanza. He runs about in the ash tree, bringing words from the eagle to Niðhöggr.

Niðhöggr is commonly known as a worm that gnaws on the roots of Yggdrasill, but his name translates as "Decapitation of the

Kinsman".... Yes, it really can translate as that! Niðhöggr is the fetus, "gnawing" on the umbilical cord (the roots of Yggdrasill) connected to the placenta.

Which can remind us of a few things, like Mímir, described as a decapitated head, and of course Óðinn himself, as the sum of the forebears, the *kinsmen*, who when he is re-born has the umbilical cord cut. The placenta is some times described as a head, Mímir, and it is indeed decapitated when Óðinn is born.

"....not many know,
where the roots run,
or how it is felled,
neither fire nor axe bites it."

Yes, because when you are born, the placenta dies, no matter what you do. Neither fire or axe kills it. The placenta kills itself: it gives itself to itself. Óðinn hanging in the tree, and falling down. Re-born.

The eagle that Ratatoskr brings words from is the same eagle we see hanging above Valhöll, as described in Grímnismál stanza 10:

"....above (Valhöll) hangs an eagle."

The eagle itself is a *complete* picture of the same: It comes from an egg and spreads out its wings (the amniotic bag). The head of the eagle is the placenta, normally located above the fetus, and it's claws are the umbilical cord attacked to the fetus. As explained in "The Secret of the She-Bear".

Ratatoskr is a squirrel. Squirrels in Europe are red. What else is red that travels between the placenta and the fetus? Blood. What is it that brings "messages" from the placenta to the fetus? Blood. What is moving fast about in the branches (the veins) of the placenta? Blood. There you have your answer. Ratatoskr is the blood.

You still don't know enough, or what?

Hamingja

"…. (Yggdrasill) stands forever green above the well of Urðr ("The Past", "Honour")"

The well of Urðr is the same as the well of Mímir ("Reminiscence"). Óðinn taps into this well, in order to "give himself to himself", in order to let past words and deeds enable him to create new words and to perform new deeds, as explained in stanza 141 in Hávamál. Before stanza 141 comes stanza 140 though, so let us quickly include that too here, just for the sake of completion:

140.
Fimbulljóð níu
nam ek af inum frægja syni
Bölþorns, Bestlu föður,
ok ek drykk of gat
ins dýra mjaðar,
ausinn Óðreri.

140.
Nine powerful songs,
I learned from the famous
son of Bölþorn ("The Bad Thorn"), Bestlá's
("The Best Liquid's") father,
and a drink I enjoyed,
of the precious mead,
that is scooped from Óðreri ("What moves
the Mind").

Do I even need to explain what that means? Don't you know enough already, to understand that? Ok, I will explain it just to be sure, even though I wish to quickly move on to the next verse: The fetus learns the "songs" (memories) of previous lives; the son of "the bad thorn", the umbilical cord, is the amniotic bag; "the best liquid" is the amniotic liquid; the precious mead is the blood of the mother, that is filtered to the fetus via the placenta (that "moves the mind").

So Óðinn has been re-incarnated, but what happens then?

141:
Þá nam ek frævask
ok fróðr vera
ok vaxa ok vel hafask,
orð mér af orði
orðs leitaði,
verk mér af verki
verks leitaði.

141.
Then I became fertile
and became wise,
I grew and thrived,
words let me on
to more words,
deeds led me on
to more deeds.

Why? Because he has transferred the "songs" of previous lives from placenta to the fetus. Óðinn, the Mind, not only lives on, but can even continue the journey through a *new* life: the words of the past let him understand more and learn new words. The deeds of the past lets him know more and enable him to perform new deeds in this life! The accumulated Honour of past lives has been transferred to him in his new body.

We could say that "the Mind travels in bodies". And that is exactly what our forebears said. They called it *Hamingja*. If you look up the word in a Norse dictionary you will find a different meaning though: "(Spirit) Double", "Follower" or "Luck". This was the name for something that gave you luck in life. Some sort of guardian angel.

However, *Hamingja* derives from the term *Ham-gengja*, that literally means "shape-walking", from *hamr* ("shape", "mind") and *genga* ("to walk"). And what was walking in shapes, in physical shapes? Yes: Óðinn. The Mind. The Honour. The accumulated Honour of your past lives.

...and this gave you luck? This protected you like a follower? This was your double? This was Óðinn in you?

In order to gain *Hamingja*, you needed to behave Honourably. It was the acts of Honour that built the *Hamingja*! So *Hamingja was* your Honour. *And* the accumulated Honour of your past lives.

142.
Rúnar munt þú finna
ok ráðna stafi,
mjök stóra stafi,
mjök stinna stafi,
er fáði fimbulþulr
ok gerðu ginnregin
ok reist hroftr rögna.

142.
You will find runes (secrets),
and interpret secrets,
big secrets,
powerful secrets,
that the great sage recorded,
that the sacred gods made
and the highest sage carved.

And your *Hamingja* is what enables you to do this... The *Honour* of this life, and *the accumulated Honour of past lives*.

But then why is it Grímnismál tells us in stanza 8 that it is those killed *by weapons* that come to Valhöll? Is something amiss again here?

Valhöll

So let us return to and explain what is said in Grímnismál:

8. Glaðsheimr heitir inn fimmti,
þars in gullbjarta Valhöll víð of þrumir;
en þar Hroftr kýss hverjan dag
vápndauða vera.

8.
The fifth is Glaðsheimr ("Fair Home"),
gold-bright there stands wide Valhöll;.
And there does Hroftr each day choose
men who have been killed with weapons.

When we know that Óðinn is the Mind, the Honour, the accumulated Honour of the past, that is being transferred from the placenta to the fetus in the womb, and Valhöll is his hall. Then Valhöll is the womb. And what happens in the womb?

Well, in order for there to be a fetus and a placenta and so forth to begin with, an egg needs to be fertilized. A sperm cell needs to be chosen by the egg. Or if you like, an egg needs to be chosen by a sperm cell. How does that happen? *It penetrates the egg....* like a spear penetrated Óðinn in the tree, right?

So yes, only those "killed with weapons", only the eggs that are penetrated by sperm cells, come to Valhöll. The others are not chosen for re-incarnation.

9. Mjök er auðkennt,
þeim er til Óðins koma
salkynni at séa;
sköftum er rann reft,
skjöldum er salr þakiðr,
brynjum um bekki strát.

9.

Easy is it to know
who to Óðinn comes
and beholds the hall
Its rafters are made of spears
the roof is covered with shields,
on the benches mail shirts are strewn

Indeed, by now it should be easy for us to know who comes to Óðinn and beholds his hall. Those who lived an Honourable life – great men and women buried with spears, shields and mail shirts in sacred mounds. This has a double meaning though: the fetus is well protected from impact by the womb of the mother. It acts as armour and a shield, and it is even called "a fortress" in French.

10. Mjök er auðkennt,
þeir er til Óðins koma
salkynni at séa:
vargr hangir fyr vestan dyrr,
ok drúpir örn yfir.

10.
Easy is it to know
who to Óðinn comes
and beholds the hall:
a wolf hangs
west of the door
above hangs an eagle.

The door to Valhöll? The door to the womb? I think we all know what that is, and just like in other myths, it is described as or linked to a wolf. See "The Secret of the She-Bear" for more on that.

The eagle hanging above is the placenta, that normally is located on top of the fetus in the womb.

18. Andhrímnir lætr í Eldhrímni
Sæhrímni soðinn, fleska bezt;
en þat fáir vitu,
við hvat einherjar alask.

18.
The cook Spirit cooks the wild boar Sea's
bacon in the cauldron Fire.
but few men know
what is nourishing those who fight alone

To nourish the fetus, to teach it the "sacred songs" of previous lives, the spirit (Óðinn) needs the fetus to "drink" the blood that comes from the placenta. The wild boar is the amniotic bag (with it's "sea", the amniotic liquid) and the placenta, feeding itself on the mother, like a wild boar feeds itself from digging into the Earth, and the cauldron is the womb. See "The Secret of the She-bear" and "Paganism Explained Part II" for more on the boar as a symbol for this.

19. Gera ok Freka seðr gunntamiðr
hróðigr Herjaföður;
en við vín eitt vápngöfugr
Óðinn æ lifir.

19.
The famous warrior father
accustomed to fighting
feeds Geri ("greedy") and Freki
("the greedy").
But on wine alone
does the weapon-fine
Óðinn ("Mind") forever live.

Who is famous? Yes, the honourable forebear is, Óðinn is. Who is "weapon-fine"? Yes, Óðinn is, he has attached himself to an egg with his spear. He does not eat anything himself though. The pregnant mother does that: the wolves. Again you see wolves as a symbol of the woman. She eats the food, and transforms it into blood for the placenta. Óðinn himself, the fetus, drinks only blood (wine). See "The Secret of the She-Bear" for more about why the symbol of the mother is some times a wolf or a dog, some times two and some times three.

20. Huginn ok Muninn fljúga hverjan dag
Jörmungrund yfir;
óumk ek of Hugin, at hann aftr né komi-t,
þó sjámk meir of Munin.

20.
The Huginn ("Mind") and Munin
("Memory")
fly every day
over the wide Earth
I fear that the Mind
does not come back
and even more I fear for the Memory.

Yes, indeed, Óðinn's mind and memory "walks in shapes" every day, over the wide Earth. You see, the Norse term for "day", *dagr*, means also "lifetime" or just "life". Every time Óðinn falls down from Yggdrasill *again*, he moves about in the world. He lives. His mind and memory is re-incarnated.

He fears though, that he will not live an Honourable life, and thus not be remembered. If he is not remembered, he will not be re-incarnated.

21. Þýtr Þund, unir Þjóðvitnis
fiskr flóði í;
árstraumr þykkir ofmikill
Valglaumni at vaða.

21.
The Swelling moans,
the great wolf's
fish swim in the flood.
The Age-old-stream seems
too big
to wade for Þjóðvitnir ("Noisy Fallen/Choosen")

More details, to those who still don't know enough. The swelling mother is being impregnated again. Sperm cells swim into her womb to find an egg. Most of them fail. The river is is too big for them to wade trough. Only one will be chosen!

22. Valgrind heitir, er stendr velli á
heilög fyr helgum dyrum;
forn er sú grind, en þat fáir vitu,
hvé hon er í lás of lokin.

22.
The Gate of the Fallen/Chosen it is called
it stands on the mound,
sacred in front of sacred doors.
Age-old is the gate
and few know
how to unlock it.

Actually, yes. Very few know what triggers a birth. Very few knows how to make a woman give birth. We still don't fully understand this today, in the year 2018.

23. Fimm hundruð dura ok umb fjórum tögum,
svá hygg ek á Valhöllu vera;
átta hundruð Einherja ganga senn ór einum durum,
þá er þeir fara við vitni at vega.

23.
Five hundred doors
and another fourty
I believe there must be in the Hall of the
Fallen/Choosen.
Eight hundred warriors fighting alone
can walk through one (each) door
when they go to fight the wolf.

How can eight hundred warriors walk through the same door at the same time, and still be said to "fight alone"? It is because they are all the same individual: all the memories of previous lives in one individual. He is all his forebears, all the accumulated Honour of his kin, but he is also alone. See stanza 24.

Fighting the wolf? That's what you do when you are born. When you pass through that one door to Valhöll, described as a wolf. Again. Like Cerebos guarding the entrance to Hades.

24. Fimm hundruð golfa ok umb fjórum
tögum,

svá hygg ek Bilskirrni með bugum;
ranna þeira, er ek reft vita,
míns veit ek mest magar.

24.

Five hundred floors
and another fourty
are built in Bilskirnir ("Wound-Cleansing")
Of all the halls
I know were built,
my son owns the biggest.

This is the birth, because 540 is (5 + 4 + 0 =)
9 , so nine months of pregnancy have
passed. Also, midwives use the fingers to
measure the opening of the cervix, to see if
the woman is ready to give birth. She is
when the opening is 8 fingers wide. 800 is
(8 + 0 + 0 =) 8. The child with all his
forebears in him can exit.

The biggest hall is of course the world
outside the womb. That he enters when he
is born.

25. Heiðrún heitir geit, er stendr höllu á
ok bítr af Læraðs limum;
skapker fylla hon skal ins skíra mjaðar;
kná-at sú veig vanask.

25.
Heiðrún ("Secret Honour") is the name
of the goat
she stands on the hall
and she gnaws on the branches of
Lærádr ("Teaching-Mind")
she fills up a vessel
with the purest mead
so that she never goes empty.

Oh, and and here we have the key that
unlocks the gate to Valhöll, mentioned in
stanza 22. Here we have an explanation to
what it is that triggers a birth: The goat
Heiðrún. This time the placenta is called
"Teaching Mind". That's what I already
said: It teaches the fetus the "songs" of
previous lives.

This goat is known from Greek mythology as Pan, from Norse as Loki, and from modern science mainly as *adrenaline*. When the adrenaline "gnaws" on the placenta, "the teaching mind", when it rushes through the blood veins, the birth is triggered.

Will the neurons producing adrenaline ever fail to produce? Can we ever run out of adrenaline? According to this stanza we cannot.

26. Eikþyrnir heitir hjörtr, er stendr höllu á
ok bítr af Læraðs limum;
en af hans hornum drýpr í Hvergelmi,
þaðan eigu vötn öll vega.

26.
The hart Eikþyrnir ("Oak-Thorns")
he stands on the hall
and bites on the branches of Læráðr
("Teaching-Mind")
From his horns
drip into Hvergelmi ("Age-old Kettle")
from there all the water comes.

The second trigger for a birth is when the child pushes its head to the inside of the cervix. Like a deer he gores his way out. He breaks the membrane of the fetus with his head, his "horns", causing the water to flow into the "age-old kettle".

The names of the rivers running are as follows:

27. Síð ok Víð, Sækin ok Eikin,
Svöl ok Gunnþró, Fjörm ok Fimbulþul,
Rín ok Rennandi, Gipul ok Göpul,
Gömul ok Geirvimul, þær hverfa um hodd
goða, Þyn ok Vín, Þöll ok Höll, Gráð ok
Gunnþorin.

27. Tradition/Custom and Wood, Brave and
Oaken, Cool and Strife-Trough, Vigorous
and Great Skald, Run and Running, Giver
and (???), The Old and Spear Swinger,
they run about the halls of the gods,
Thin and Wine, Toll/Duty and Slope,
Greed and Torn-by-Strife.

28. Vína heitir ein, önnur Vegsvinn,
þriðja Þjóðnuma, Nyt ok Nöt,
Nönn ok Hrönn, Slíð ok Hríð,
Sylgr ok Ylgr, Víð ok Ván,
Vönd ok Strönd, Gjöll ok Leiftr,
þær falla gumnum nær, er falla til Heljar
heðan.

28. Girlfriend one is called, another Road-
Wise, the third People-Stealer, Good Use
and Spear, Brave and Heap-of-Stones,
Terrible/Tired and Ride/Storm,
Swallow/Drink and She-Wolf, Metal-
Ring/The-Two-of-Us and Hope,
Difficult and River-Bed/Beach,
Resound/Echo and Shining Light,
they fall to men, they fall down to Hel
("Hidden", "Hall").

These rivers are what pushes him into the
world, into life. They are the qualities or
abilities what will keep him alive. For some
time...

29. Körmt ok Örmt ok Kerlaugar tvær,
þær skal Þórr vaða dag hvern,
er hann dæma ferr at aski Yggdrasils,
því at ásbrú brenn öll loga,
heilög vötn hlóa.

29. Körmt (?) and Örmt (?) and the Twins of
the Tub Bath
Þórr shall each day wade through
when to give judgement he shall go to the
ash tree Yggdrasill ("the terrible horse")
Because of that the spirit-bridge
shall burn in flames
and the sacred water flow.

The twins of the tub bath (the womb) are
the fetus and it's "twin" the placenta, as
explained in detail in "The Secret of the
She-Bear". Þórr ("Thunder") is the spark of
life, the life-force that we all lose at some
point, after the day (life) ends, and that
comes back to us when we are reborn.
When he "goes to the womb of the mother"
again, when he "hangs" in Yggdrasill, the
placenta. The spirit-bridge that burns in

flames is the cervix that turns red from blood (fire) when the mother gives birth. And yes, she will give birth when her water flows...

The cervix is indeed a bridge for the spirits. This is how Óðinn can return to life. This is his bridge from memory to physical form.

30. Glaðr ok Gyllir, Glær ok Skeiðbrimir, Silfrintoppr ok Sinir, Gísl ok Falhófnir, Gulltoppr ok Léttfeti, þeim ríða æsir jóm dag hvern, er þeir dæma fara at aski Yggdrasils.

30. Fair and Golden, Sea and Fire-Race/Fire-Run, Silver-Hair and Strong, Guardian and Dead-Hoofs, Golden-Hair and Light Footed, the Æsir ("Spirits") ride every day, when they travel to the ash Yggdrasill ("The Terrible Horse").

In order to re-incarnate, all the gods need to ride their "horses", that all describe the placenta, and help you understand the meaning also of the other myths, where the same symbols are used (e. g. the long golden hair being the umbilical cord in the fairy tale called Rapunzel). They are The Terrible Horse, Yggdrasill. The horse as a symbol for the placenta is described in detail in "The Secret of the She-bear".

Do you know enough now, or what? Do you still need to know more to understand what Valhöll is?

Óðinn ek nú heiti...

At this point I will ask you to please read the last stanza of Grímnismál, and tell me if you don't understand what it means by now:

54.

Óðinn ek nú heiti,
Yggr ek áðan hét,
hétumk Þundr fyr þat,
Vakr ok Skilfingr,
Váfuðr ok Hroftatýr,
Gautr ok Jalkr með goðum,
Ófnir ok Sváfnir,
er ek hygg, at orðnir sé
allir af einum mér.

54.

My name is now Óðinn,
Yggr used to be my name,
my name was Þundr before that,
Vakr and Skilfingr,
Váfuðr and Hroftatýr,
Gautr and Jalkr amongst gods,

Ófnir and Sváfnir,
all of these, I believe,
have become me alone.

Note:
Yggr ("The Terrible"),
Þundr ("Swell"),
Vakr ("Woke"),
Skilfingr ("Separating-Finger"),
Váfuðr ("Wanderer"),
Hroftatýr ("Sage God"),
Gautr ("Boaster"),
Jalkr ("Castrated Horse"),
Ófnir ("Warmer"),
Sváfnir ("Cooler").

This is a summing up of the whole process
of re-incarnation.... the 10 lunar months of
prengancy. First he is connected to the
placenta (Yggr), then the mother's womb
swell up (Þundr), then the fetus becomes
alive, his heart and mind wakes up (Vákr),
then his body developes (Skilfingr), he
starts to move (Váfuðr), he learns from
Mímir (Hroftatýr), he is born and screams

(Gautr), the umbilical cord is cut (Jalkr) and the child moves from the warm womb (Ófnir) to the cold world (Sváfnir).

At the same time, the listing of names Óðinn used to have, explains how he is the sum of previous lives.

"...all of these, I believe,
have become me alone."

He is what he has gone through. In this life. In past lives. And in the world in the middle: In the mother's womb.

Had you known those passwords from the beginning, you could have understood everything about this process from this one single stanza alone...

Conclusion

Now we can tell why Óðinn is said to have had hundreds of names. At least most of them are names that he had in previous lives. He has fallen from Yggdrasill *hundreds* of times. Each time he is re-incarnated he becomes himself alone, and at the same time he is the sum of all his previous lives. The sum of the Honour accumulated in all his previous lives.

But Óðinn is *you*.... we are all Óðinn. The mythology tells us that we have lived before, hundreds of times. At times it explains how we remember those previous lives from Mímir in the womb of the mother. Other times it explains how we awaken the memories as 7-8 year old children entering burial mounds or visiting sacred trees or beholding the sacred objects we used to own in previous lives.

But always, whether it is from this angle or that angle, in this way or that way, it describes a re-incarnation. They never dreamt of an "eternal afterlife" in some "Heavenly Paradise". They had no such contempt for life or superstitions. Instead they believed in re-incarnation and an Honourable life on Earth.

Sources for this book:

-*Samlagets Norrøn ordbok*, 5. utgåva, Oslo 2012

-Snorri Sturluson's *The Eddas*;

> Grímnismál

> Hávamál

> Völuspá

-Hjalmar Falk's, *Etymologisk Ordbog over det norske og det danske Sprog*, Kristiania 1906.

Other books by Varg Vikernes

-*Vargsmål*, Oslo 1997

-*Germansk Mytologi og Verdensanskuelse*, Stockholm 2000

-*Sorcery and Religion in Ancient Scandinavia*, London 2011

-*Reflections on European Mythology and Polytheism*, 2015

-*Mythic Fantasy Role-playing Game (MYFAROG) v. 2.6*, 2015

Other books by Marie Cachet

-*Le secret de l'Ourse*, 2016

-*Le besoin d'impossible*, 2009

Made in the USA
Las Vegas, NV
26 August 2024

94484933R00036